# Mapping the Way

by Jeff O'Kelley

**buildings**

**country**

**map**

**road**

**street**

**town**

A map is a drawing. A map shows you where places are. A map helps you find places.

▲ Look at this park.

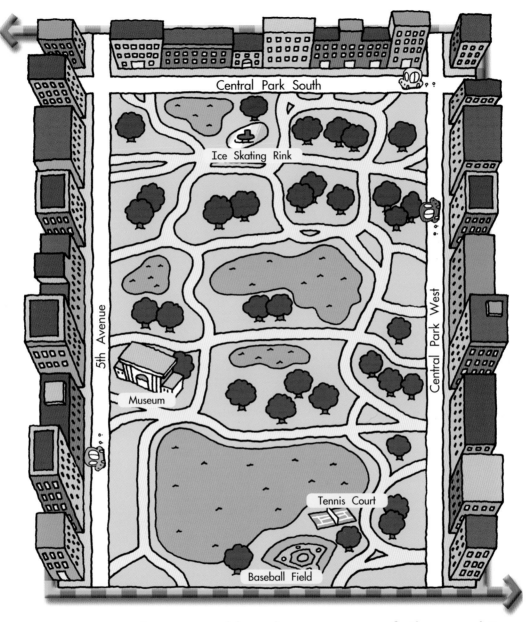

Central Park South

Ice Skating Rink

5th Avenue

Central Park West

Museum

Tennis Court

Baseball Field

▲ How is the map like the picture of the park?

This town is on a map.

This map shows the same town.
You can find streets or roads.
You can find buildings. You can
find many places.

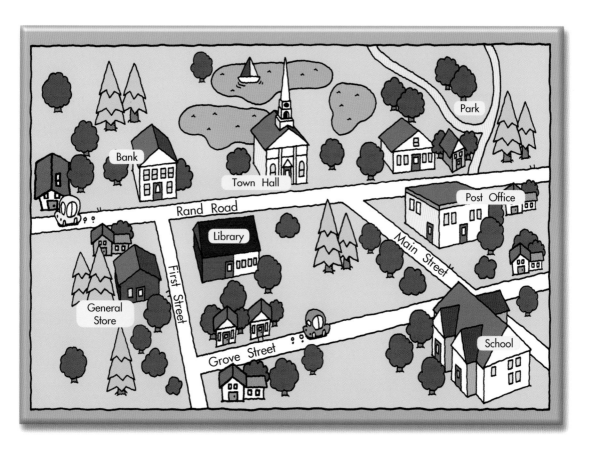

▲ Look at the names of the buildings.

You can find a place on the map.
Find Main Street on the map.

▲ Look at the street names.

Now, find a place on Main Street.
Can you find the school?

Park

Post Office

Main Street

School

▲ What other places
are on the map?

Can you find the park on the map? Start at the school. How can you get to the park?

Bank

Town Hall

Rand Road

Library

First Street

General Store

Grove Street

The map can help you. The map can show you how to get to the park.

Some maps show a town.
Some maps show a country.

Map of a Town

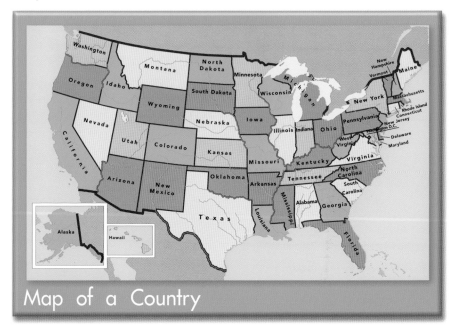

Map of a Country

This map shows North America.
Can you find your country on
the map?

Map of North America

This map shows the United States.
Two oceans are on the map.

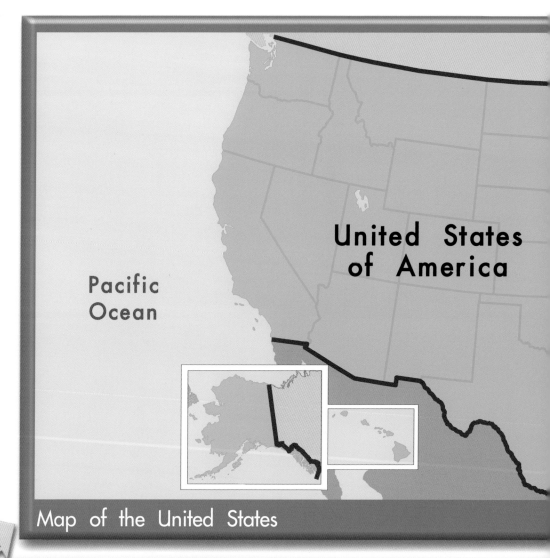

Pacific
Ocean

United States
of America

Map of the United States

The map shows the Atlantic Ocean on the right. The map shows the Pacific Ocean on the left. Can you find the oceans?

Atlantic
Ocean

The map of the United States shows many places. Where do you want to go?

1 Golden Gate Bridge
2 Arches National Park
3 Mount Rushmore
4 Gateway Arch
5 Sears Tower
6 The Everglades
7 Capitol Hill
8 Statue of Liberty